Loft

DESIGN | DECOR

Editor: **Jennifer Eiss**
Translator: **Krister Swartz**
Interior Designer: **Eleonore Gerbier**
Layout: **Nord Compo**

Library of Congress Cataloging-in-Publication Data is on file with the Library of Congress.

ISBN-13: 978–1–58479–556–8
ISBN-10: 1–58479–556–5

The text of this book was composed in Gill Sans and Stone Sans

Printed and bound in Spain
10 9 8 7 6 5 4 3 2 1

harry n. abrams, inc.
a subsidiary of La Martinière Groupe
115 West 18th Street
New York, NY 10011
www.hnabooks.com

Loft

Philippe Saharoff & Inès Heugel

D E S I G N | **D E C O R**

Stewart, Tabori & Chang
New York

Foreword

The loft is a living space founded on the idea of volume, of a refuge from the standard domestic layout of one room, one function, and of utilizing rough material like steel and concrete. It has an air of freedom, of a place where everyone can express his personality and his originality, rejecting the tyranny of good taste and traditional ideas about housing.

The loft trend already has a history. It was born in New York, back in the 1950s. At that time, many factories and manufacturers in Manhattan closed their doors, which led to the migration of the middle class from the city center to the suburbs. Artists avid for room to work took over these immense abandoned spaces, which offered no heat or comfort. They transformed these work spaces and alternative living spaces into poles of attraction that, in their turn, appealed to intellectuals and professionals. A choice of housing that started as a way to express independence and display an antiestablishment tendency, little by little, shifted to become the embodiment of an aesthetic ideal.

From its New York beginnings, the loft movement has spread to other large cities of America and Europe, notably London, Antwerp, and Paris. Today, it is not merely a choice of living space but a social phenomenon, truly creating its own market. Old factories, warehouses, workshops, art studios, and storefront spaces, as well as garages, schools, and even churches, have all been transformed into lofts. Real estate agents now propose plans for the conversion of properties, pulling down interior walls in apartments and turning them into miniature "lofts"; anything can be called a loft, as long as it lacks partitions.

The loft has come to embody an art of living that is in tune with the spirit of our era, and destined to leave its mark on all living spaces. Its grand principles are freedom, openness, flexibility, and the nomadic way of life.

The Living Space

The theoretical absence of partitions in a loft creates a vast, flexible living space. It is this that determines our vision of the loft lifestyle, and all of our essential questions. What flooring will you choose? Do you want to warm up your loft with wooden floors, go for an industrial feel by choosing concrete, or just lay down a simple linoleum floor? Do you want to put in a fireplace? Can you? Are you going to preserve the rough style of your loft by leaving brick walls, water pipes, and heating ducts visible, or conceal all of this by boxing it in and meticulously painting it? All of this is a matter of taste. A bit of advice: always remember that, unlike ordinary apartments, a loft often boasts a special history, and it may give you satisfaction to let some evocative elements of its past remain visible, though it's not necessary to go so far as making a museum out of your loft.

You must also think of the organization of the loft. If you have a family, it is convenient to create intimate spaces for parents and children and to demarcate the zones of activity—television corner, work space, eating area, and so on—while retaining the spirit of freedom inherent in the loft. If you don't want to fragment the space, why not use movable partitions in the form of furniture or modular shelving, accessible on both sides? These could be outfitted with casters, and hold books or decorative objects. You can also define spaces with a large modular sofa, or an area rug. Perhaps you might make an office or TV corner with a loft, a platform, or a mezzanine. Instead of hanging paintings or photos on the wall, why not arrange them on little shelves, to be frequently changed? The art of converting a loft is in finding original responses to specific questions posed by the space; it is in reinventing the art of living, on the principles of freedom and flexibility.

FLOORS

Covering a floor can use up a significant part of your budget. A mistake here will be even more costly than in other areas, because you can't simply add a new layer of paint, as you can with a wall. You will need to find solutions that are both economical and aesthetically appealing, and to choose material that combines solidity, longevity, and comfort. Wood and stone remain the obvious choices, but the spirit of the loft allows for more industrial solutions like concrete, linoleum, rubber, or even metal. Even more than in other areas, it might be a good idea to turn to a professional for flooring.

WOOD FLOORS

The most popular choice for wood-plank floors is oak, but hardwood floors come in many kinds of durable wood, which feature a range of colors and grains—mahogany, birch, beech, maple, and chestnut, for example.

Soft woods like redwood, pine, fir, or spruce are less heavy, less solid, and need some kind of treatment against rotting. Exotic woods like teak, iroko, or merbau are at once durable and relatively easy to live with. For lofts, wide planks, six to eight inches wide, are particularly spectacular, but they cost more. You might track down old floorboards from a demolished building or gymnasium at a salvage dealer. These are solid and have an antique look that is very pleasant. Installation, which really should be done by a professional, can sometimes become expensive, because the boards have to be leveled. If you don't have a lot to spend, ask your finish carpenter to simply lay the boards, instead of using a more sophisticated method such as tongue and groove; the rough look of a loft makes such refinement unnecessary. The treatment most often used now, which requires the least maintenance, is coating the floor with a durable finish like polyurethane. This is available these days in a more natural satin finish, if you don't want high gloss. Be careful: many of these finishes can darken the wood. Wax or oil is inadvisable; certainly the look is unbeatable, but it doesn't stand up to heavy wear, and will have to be reapplied several times a year. You can also paint, bleach, or apply a pickled or color-washed finish to your wood floor. Wood flooring is available in thinner strips that are very economical and very easy to maintain, as they have already been finished, and sometimes even insulated. They come in a large array of wood types and colors, and can be veneer or laminated wood. In addition, they are easy to install, as they fit together without nails or adhesive.

STONE FLOORS

There are great many advantages to stone: it is solid, it wears well, and it needs little care, apart from a preliminary sealing treatment to prevent it becoming porous. Because it holds heat well, it also makes a good choice to lay over an under-floor heating system. Due to its great weight, however, it is probably best used only for the ground floor, and it is also relatively expensive. You can opt for a durable stone like granite or for softer types, like limestone or sandstone. Slate is currently trendy; it is waterproof, and doesn't show dirt. It usually comes in slabs pretreated with a sealant—if not, you will need to seal it after installing. Reconstituted stone, made with a molded mixture of concrete and minerals, can be an interesting alternative, and its regular dimensions makes it much easier to install. It can be laid in various patterns: a pinwheel pattern is formed by a group of four rectangular stones at right angles to each other, surrounding a smaller square stone, repeated in a grid; a broken bond alternates stones of the same width but different lengths; and a herringbone pattern is made with stones laid on the diagonal.

1 The clean lines of aluminum flooring, installed in a high-traffic area.
2 This parquet floor of exotic wood is animated by the varying colors of the individual strips.
3 To define the different areas of this loft, concrete has been tinted, polished, and ornamented with metal studs and dotted lines.

FLEXIBLE FLOOR COVERINGS

If your budget is limited, don't hesitate to think about flexible floor coverings; anything goes in a loft. Look through all of the catalogs. There is a wide range of colors and designs to choose from; it would be a considerable surprise if you didn't find something you liked. Vinyl is easy on your feet. For a high-traffic area, like a living room, choose a heavy, thick vinyl. Remember, the thicker the flooring, the more solid it is, and the more shock it will absorb. Vinyl comes in square tiles or in large sheets. You can choose from solids, terrazzo effects, or checkerboards, or you can design an effect like a carpet. Vinyl is also the king of faux: designs that imitate parquet, marble, brick, stone, and so on can inject an irreverent, even humorous, touch. This is also true of linoleum, which is made of a mixture of cork powder, linseed oil, and resin, pressed into a jute backing and fused together at high temperatures. This can be bought in square tiles or large sheets. If you choose linoleum tiles, you will have to lay them perfectly; any unevenness in the floor can make it very difficult to achieve a tight fit. Rubber, available in tiles or rolls, can have a lovely effect in a loft. Since it appeared in the Milan Metro in the 1930s, rubber ornamented with raised ribs or lozenges has been adopted in a number of industrial settings. Its principal virtues are its solidity,

insulating qualities, and impermeability. But rubber has two drawbacks: dust settles easily in grooves or cracks in it, and it stains easily. The tiles can be laid without adhesive, but this is not recommended; for a living room, use an acrylic adhesive.

CONCRETE FLOORS

It's partly due to the loft phenomenon that concrete has become so sought after as a stylish floor material. But, be forewarned, it is a material that demands skilled labor. A mixture of cement, water, and sand, concrete needs to cure for six to twenty days after pouring, and it must be poured all at once.

The classic concrete is rough and gray. It displays the irregular marks of the wood frame it was poured into, which might be of softwood laths, metal, or plastic. If you find its uncompromising gray to be a little austere, you can tint concrete. For the most part, this is done while the concrete is still wet, using natural or artificial pigments, or colored sand. You can also color your concrete's surface by sprinkling pigment over it, which gives it an irregular, marbleized look. In both cases, it is imperative that you seal it with a protective coating. Finally, concrete can be painted with quick-drying paint.

For a glossier finish on your concrete floor, polish it either when the floor is still wet, manually or with a special machine, or when the floor is dry, by using a power buffer. The more the surface is polished, the more shine it will have. For an amusing effect, other materials—wood, stoneware, stones, or pebbles—can be incorporated into a concrete floor.

1 Easy to maintain, this laminated flooring is a marvelous imitation of exotic wood parquet.

2 A polished concrete floor gives this immense area, animated by a mezzanine balcony, a resolutely industrial look.

COLOR

Everyone knows that deep colors make a room seem smaller, whereas light hues make it seem bigger; that a dark ceiling makes it seem lower; and that matte surfaces absorb light and appear darker than glossy surfaces. For a floor, the light, glossy and solid colors make the room seem bigger, just as dark, matte colors and designs make it smaller.

Not all colors go together. If you have a large space, it is better to choose subtle, neutral colors, because bright colors over large areas can fatigue the eye. To avoid mistakes, it is better to choose one base color and then vary its shades.

You can also play with two contrasting colors, for example gray and red or even green and brick: in this case, choose a dominant color and a contrasting hue with the same value. If you want to tackle more subtle color combinations, take your cue from a painting or a carpet that you like, survey photographs of Tuscan or Mexican architecture or Scandinavian interior design, or leaf through books on painting. Once you have

chosen your colors, before you begin, be sure to make test patches on a few important surfaces.

If you are worried that you may grow tired of the colors you've chosen, you might want to stick to a soft palette of natural colors. Straw, off-white, cream, fawn, light gray, and beige are simple, restful, and won't wear on the eye. And, of course, there is pure white, which is especially valuable because it brings out other colors; a carpet, a sofa slipcover, furniture, and above all, works of art can glow against a white background. It can also be fun to use color to underline or bring out the architectural aspects of a loft, its industrial side. Generally, this means using pale or neutral colors for the most part and emphasizing columns, gangways, or metal beams with gray, black, or some other contrasting color. Finally, a subtle but effective way to evade the monotony of a monochrome color scheme is to combine matte paint, on the walls, for example, with gloss paint on the ceiling and columns.

1 A harmony of reds and yellows makes for a stimulating living space.
2 A severe graphic design against a radiant wall.

1

FIREPLACES AND HEATERS

In order to keep your loft warm economically, you will need to pay careful attention to insulation: doors and windows have to be absolutely tight-fitting. Once this has been taken care of, you can choose between radiant under-floor heating, which is very nice and can be installed under all types of flooring (concrete, stone, or wood) and traditional central heating. Some industrial radiators are very stylish. In their very pure functional design, they can resemble contemporary sculpture: look for sleek flat-panel radiators and those with vividly colored metallic pipes, or columns of shining metal. You can also salvage an old cast-iron heater that asks nothing but to serve. But for real ambience, you may want to install a fireplace. Its size should be, of course, in pro-portion to the dimensions of the loft. In a large living space, a double-faced fireplace, which gives off natural light, heats the spaces on both sides; the same goes for a free-standing fireplace, which can be efficient and neat. If you prefer your fireplace against a wall, you might find an old mantelpiece in stone, wood, or marble. But you could also design one according to your dreams. In an old workshop space, brick can produce a nice effect. But there is nothing to prevent you from using ceramic tile, cast iron, metal, or stone.

An alternative to the traditional fireplace is the wood-burning or coal-burning stove. You can open the doors to view the fire, and close them when you leave the room.

1 This freestanding double-sided fireplace has the advantage of heating both sides of the room.

2 In the center of a room, this wood stove has a clean, functional look.

3 Large industrial radiators run along a glass wall.

LIGHTING

Since enlarging a window, creating a picture window, or installing a skylight is not always possible in a loft, the natural light that exists should be optimized. To begin with, remove all opaque partitions—at least those that are not movable—and replace them with translucent partitions, of glass bricks, for example, or sliding panels of paper or light cloth. Transparent or open storage spaces (for example, bookshelves that only run halfway up to the ceiling and thereby let light pass over them) are also welcome. Think also of how gloss paint reflects light, and how a well-placed mirror can throw light into a room.

If your loft gets natural light on one side only, you might want to light the opposite side with concealed fluorescent tubes or neon. Don't be afraid that this lighting, which has served well since its invention in the nineteenth century, will transform your cozy nest into an institutional dining room. It produces a light very similar to that of natural light.

For nighttime, good lighting is accomplished by combining many sources of light. You must first supply ambient lighting, which can come from flush-fitting ceiling and/or wall lights; from spotlights with low-wattage bulbs installed in a drop ceiling, on tracks, or on columns equipped with swiveling spotlights at different heights; or from fluorescent tubes. Low-wattage bulbs are very economical, and can light an entire wall. By installing a dimmer switch, you can modulate this ambient light according to your needs or activities.

Once you have created this adjustable basic lighting, turn your mind to localized sources of light to brighten a reading corner, a desk, a work area, or a dining table, or to highlight some work of art. Choose adjustable lamps or spotlights aimed at specific objects. Finally, to add a more personal touch to your lighting, add a sculptural lamp by your favorite designer, a floor lamp found at a flea market, or the chandelier of your dreams, and complete the setting with candelabra and sconces.

1 Wall sconces and table lamps in a loft inundated with natural light.

2 The ideal lighting: natural light throughout the day, spotlights mounted on rails and standing lamps for use at night.

1 A beautiful designer lamp gives a nod to the contemporary triptych that decorates the wall.

2 A garland of light hangs beside a wood support column, lighting up the loft from top to bottom.

3 In a romantic spirit, hanging lamps with pleated cloth shades.

4 The paned screen, the wood of the stairs, and the large fabric lamp make a soft and warm ensemble.

OFFICE SPACE

It is not easy to find a corner in a loft where you can work in peace. Depending on the organization of your space and the hours its inhabitants keep, you might be able to arrange work space in an attic room, on a mezzanine, in a corner of the living area. Once you've found the right spot, you will know it. The advantage of working at home is that you can personalize your office so that it resembles no other. To start with, you will need a desk or table. An old workshop or factory table could serve, or an old wooden or metal table, or a slab of glass or a simple plank on trestles. If you have natural light, place the desk to one side of a window, or in front of it, if the sun doesn't shine straight in—if the light is coming from behind you, your shadow might get in the way. You will also need a comfortable chair.

There are some nice old wooden swivel chairs, but you don't have to have a real desk chair: there are all kinds of nice chairs to buy. A good articulated lamp completes the ambience.

Then there is the important question of storage. If you have opted for a desk, you will have some drawers where you can store your supplies. But this will probably not be enough. You will certainly need to install a small bookcase with both open and closed shelves near your work table, or even shelved units on easy-to-move casters. Office furniture, storage units from do-it-yourself stores, racks, and wicker or metal baskets offer storage for all of your materials. And there's nothing to stop you from personalizing the place with your photos, paintings, and art objects.

1

1 A basement office is illuminated by a light well cut underneath the bay window of the living room.

2 In a workspace installed on a mezzanine blessed with plenty of natural light, the furniture and closed storage space display clean, pure lines.

3 Against a rough stone wall, a desktop and simple shelf storage.

THE LIBRARY

As with all storage spaces, it is a good idea to first make a little inventory and calculate the number of linear feet your books will take up. Divide them into categories: novels, coffee-table books, encyclopedias and dictionaries, travel guides and books about places around the world, histories, detective novels, and so on. Take advantage of this sorting to get rid of all those books you know you will never reread. Place your reference books and those that you consult regularly within reach, and find a good place to display the most attractive books.

After this, there are many ways to go. The classic approach is to cover an entire wall with your books. In a loft, this can cut a fine figure. Attach vertical supports of wood or metal to the wall, so you can install the shelves at a spacing that matches the height of your books. If need be, be sure to provide for a sound system or television. To allow you to reach books on high shelves, add a library ladder that slides along a rail.

Another solution is to distribute several collections of books around the loft where they are most needed. For example, place your cookbooks in the kitchen or near it, travel books in a work space, coffee-table books on a large table, and so on. You can also store books in large modular units, in tall narrow bookcases, or in hinged cabinets that can fold closed. If possible, set everything on casters. Bookcases that are not too high, also mounted on casters, can act as dividers between two areas of a loft without blocking the natural light. Make sure these are deep enough to hold two rows of books, to be reached from each side of the shelves. Not only will you then have a large number of books at hand, but since your shelves are not too high, you can place objects, lamps, and such on top of them. Combine open and closed units that allow you to show off what you want seen and hide the rest. And don't forget, no matter what you do, to leave plenty of room for more books!

1 Shelves arranged in a regular pattern make up this traditional library.
2 At waist height, books and magazines are in easy reach.

3 Industrial metal structures made of salvaged racks that once held meals on a Boeing 747.

SOFAS AND ARMCHAIRS

It can be very pleasant to have a large sofa, and even better to have a modular system with corner units, straight units, and units with armrests. Two or three sofas face to face or at right angles to each other can also make entertaining enjoyable. They can, moreover, serve to define an area within a large living space without the use of partitions. If your sofas are not new, you can revive them with two slipcovers; a flannel, herringbone, or woolen one for the winter, and another for summer, in linen or cotton.

As, theoretically, you are not pressed to find space, think also of roomy armchairs you can curl up in, unless you have a weakness for those lovely old club chairs or yearn for your grandmother's wingback chair. Don't hesitate to mix chairs of different styles to break the monotony. Complete the whole thing with footstools, footrests, and piles of large cushions. Group sofas and armchairs around a focal point, generally a fireplace or a coffee table, and rearrange them frequently. If you have a particularly large space, you can allow for several seating areas: one for watching television, another for a card table, a third for reading.

1 Near the fireplace, a leather and tubular metal armchair from the 1930s.
2 Rattan chairs and houseplants give an extra note of cheer to this bright, appealing space.
3 How to create an island of warmth: a sofa with an ethnic flavor, cushions, a richly colored carpet, and a wood stove.
4 A modern chair makes a harmonious if unexpected pair with an antique armchair in front of an enormous contemporary lamp.
5 Traditional comfort in leather-covered club chairs.

3

4

5

TABLES, SHELVES, AND CABINETS

If you live in an old workshop or factory, you will surely want to track down some furniture that evokes industrial or artistic activity. You will find, at the salvage stores or the specialist secondhand shops, a variety of furniture with real style: metallic pigeonholes from old post offices, print shop furniture, large drafting tables, workbenches of all kinds, cutting tables, old ice chests converted into cupboards, good solid desks, work chairs of various heights. Unrestored, these are still affordable. As for storage units or bookshelves, you can use factory or warehouse shelves. The pieces of reclaimed commercial work furniture that can be sometimes found at boutiques can also be appealing, and very functional with their multiple drawers and shelves. These can include pharmacy furniture, drapers' counters, bakers' shelves, accountants' files, and bins from feed stores, haberdashers, and so on.

THE ART OF ORGANIZATION

Make a distinction between closed storage units and open. Reserve closed units for all the objects that are not particularly attractive to look at. In a living room, avoid banal cabinets; think instead of Grandma's old chest of drawers, a sideboard found at a flea market, a chest or armoire brought back from a trip from abroad, or a nice piece of commercial furniture. To store collections of small objects and protect them from dust, think about cupboards with glazed doors, glass-topped coffee tables with a display compartment below, and glass display cabinets. For the rest, what about simple linear shelves, consoles, open cabinets, and small storage units originally used for merchandise in stores?

1 This commercial storage unit with its many drawers, freshly painted, has found a new life in a private home.

2 A coffee table resting on old railcar wheels has an air as mischievous as the eye of the portrait hanging above it is severe.

3 Here everything is stored in honey-colored boxes, carefully organized and neatly labeled.

1

2

The Kitchen and the Dining Area

Instead of using different rooms for separate functions, loft dwellers prefer an open multifunctional space that lets them be comfortable as a family and with friends. Everyone takes part in making the meal and washing up afterward. An aperitif is offered before an informal meal. Children—who, it is well known, love to be underfoot in the kitchen—are in constant contact with their parents. Quite often, this area is so nice that everyone lingers here. If the table is large, the children do their homework at it; parents have coffee or bring their computer there. In short, the kitchen/dining area becomes the soul of the house and the center of life.

But let's not forget about the small inconveniences that are part of this utopian vision. Exposed to everyone's eyes, the kitchen must be clean and well arranged. It's also important to prevent excessive noise and odor. Fortunately, these problems are not insuperable. An intermediate solution consists of separating the kitchen area from the eating area with storage units, a sideboard, or a counter, high enough to hide the work areas from view. The family table can also be integrated as a piece of furniture on the edge of the living room. To get rid of odors, a good range hood is indispensable, but make sure it is not too loud. Think also of choosing a dishwasher that is as quiet as possible.

Everything is a matter of taste. Some like their kitchen organized in straight lines, with utensils concealed in cupboards; others prefer to have everything visible and at hand. Between these two solutions, you, like most inhabitants of lofts, will most likely choose the sensible intermediate option, which consists of concealing those objects that are not as pretty or as often used, and letting the other objects be visible and easy to lay your hands on. When all is said and done, the chief imperatives for a kitchen, open or not, in a loft or not, are always the same: use good materials, install good lighting, and equip your space with suitable cabinets and work counters. Make sure, however, that the eating area is the most harmonious junction possible between the kitchen and the living area.

FLOORS

If you want to use the same flooring throughout the entire loft space, special treatment may be necessary for the area used for the kitchen. If you have decided on concrete, for example, you will need to seal it with a waterproofing product to protect the surface against stains and dampness. Failing that, cover the floor with a waterproof acrylic resin. Remember that polished concrete is delicate: it should be maintained regularly and carefully. If you simply must have a wood floor in this area, coat it with a tough, waterproof finish like polyurethane. Tropical species like teak, which withstand moisture particularly well, should still be treated and maintained to avoid stains.

The kitchen floor is constantly stressed. Perhaps it would be best, if you don't want to make your life a misery, to install a floor that can stand up to this wear and tear: in a large surface devoid of partitions, a different flooring can also effectively set off different areas. Choose floor materials that are as smooth as possible, so as not to hold dirt. Tiled floors are among the most functional; but not just any kind of tile will do. It should be resistant to wear and tear, shock, and chemicals, be waterproof, and above all the tiles should fit together tightly. Stone or slate are also very durable, but need to be coated with a linseed oil and turpentine mixture. Some flexible flooring coverings, like rubber, vinyl, or linoleum, are resistant and easy to maintain, as long as the pieces have been fit together tightly to make a perfectly level surface.

1 A harmonious juxtaposition of wood and zinc flooring.
2 This little kitchen has a floor of particle board.

3 Here a wood floor has been treated with a clear finish so it's easy to maintain.
4 The Zen ambience of this kitchen and eating area is highlighted by a carefully polished concrete floor.

3

4

STORAGE

Before installing your cabinets, make an inventory of all of your dishes, appliances, and utensils. Place them where they will be used: for example, pots and pans near the oven, a cutting board and knives near the work space, and so on. There are two kinds of storage units: closed units and open ones. If your oven is not under the kitchen counter, the ideal location for pots and pans is a large drawer. If it is deep enough, you can attach a plastic bar to the inside parallel to the door to store bottles—oil, vinegar, soy sauce, and such—used for cooking. You'll also need to have a series of racks where you can store your lids and small utensils.

There are very clever systems for storing things in cupboards: think of telescoping drawers, or of lazy Susans in the corners, for example.

RECYCLED STORAGE SOLUTIONS

Some wooden toolboxes make nice closed storage units. You can put fruits and vegetables in crates, in wooden planters, or on wicker racks; buckets, ewers, and wooden kegs can serve to hold accessories. All kinds of baskets are welcome, whether in wicker, wood, or metal; even bicycle panniers or those used in the hospital can be of some use. Glass, ceramic, or stainless steel jars are bound to find a use. And, in a loft, you can happily get away with warehouse trays on casters, metal luggage racks, shop storage units, or even a supermarket cart.

1 Floor and wall cabinets in wood, with stainless steel bars to hang utensils from.

2 These clever cabinets spell out the word EAT.

2

For open storage units, where you can have everything within reach and visible, there are two possibilities. A draining rack for dishes can be placed near or even over the sink. Think of metal rails or racks; of sheets of perforated metal on which to hang hooks to hold all the objects and utensils you often use; of glass rails, like the ones you see in bistros; of plate display units; and of salvaged banister rails on which you can hang dish towels and other utensils. Don't forget to have some vertical space to slip in some cutting boards and trays.

1 Open shelves surround a refrigerator.
2 In this old fire station without natural light, a great deal of attention to lighting was necessary.
3 These utensils are easy to reach, and attractive to the eye.

THE CENTRAL ISLAND

If you have enough space to accommodate it, a central island is a good solution. It can take on many functions. It can be used as a sideboard or workspace, or entirely as a storage unit, or even serve as a place to put your dishwasher or a small refrigerator. Or it can be used as a table on the living room side, and on the kitchen side hold drawers for storage. It can also hold an oven or cooktop.

THE COOKING ISLAND

It is much more pleasant to cook in an open space than with your nose against the wall. But some installations need electricity, and perhaps even gas, as well as a range hood whose fan and ducts must be concealed behind a dropped ceiling, at least when you are not recycling the

air. The ideal is to be able to store pots and pans as well as indispensable ingredients for cooking in this island, so that they are always close at hand.

THE DINING ISLAND

An island used for this purpose doesn't require plumbing and electricity, so it can be mounted on casters, and will afford room for numerous drawers or shelves. It is always best, for convenience's sake, to use open shelves so you don't have the added weight of doors. A good solution: install shelves on the kitchen side, and on the living room side have a semicircular tabletop that can be used as a workspace. At least be sure that the countertop projects beyond the storage units; if you do this, you can place barstools all around the island.

1 This island forms a long work counter, with room for all the dishes under it.

2 An island equipped with a stove and a sink allows for the installation of traditional storage units all around this kitchen nook.

1

1

COUNTERTOPS

Stainless steel, the champion of professional kitchens, returns in force in private homes. It is durable, very resistant, and does not warp. Its industrial look and its color make it a material very appropriate for a loft. You can also give it a warmer look by combining it with wood or granite.

Synthetic countertop materials have all the necessary qualities: they are resistant, odorless, waterproof, scratchproof, nonporous, and can withstand high heat and chemical products. In addition, they are soft to the touch and easy to maintain. The one drawback is that they are expensive.

Marble and granite have a beautiful look, come in a variety of colors, and withstand all kinds of thermal and mechanical stress. They make excellent countertops, as long as they are protected with a waterproof sealant when installed and once every year thereafter. But they are not within everyone's means.

For a more traditional look, you can opt for ceramic tiles, which are hygienic and easy to maintain. Their only weakness is that they can break if a heavy object falls on them.

Hard woods, like teak and beech, require a lot of care and thus are not recommended. On the other hand, plywood and high-pressure laminated board work well and are a relatively cheap solution.

1 This long kitchen has a professional look.
2 A festival of materials: rough brick, stone, wood, and ceramic tile.
3 Looking out on nature, a countertop in wood with a steel sink and a space-efficient shallow cooktop.
4 Tiled flooring and wood in this garret kitchen.

2

3

4

LIGHTING

To light a kitchen well, you need to follow the same principles that hold for the rest of the loft: combine ambient light with direct light. The first can come from the ceiling, from low-wattage spotlights integrated in a drop ceiling or suspended from cables, or large spotlights fixed in the ceiling in groups of two or three. Direct lighting should be placed over workspaces, to do away with shadows. Even better would be to run lighting under tall furniture, in the form, of fluorescent tubes, for example. Above the dining area, one or many suspended light sources—like nautical or industrial lamps—can serve well, unless you prefer a classic chandelier, which in a loft can produce a beautiful and unexpected effect.

1 In this kitchen with open storage shelves, a large industrial metal hanging lamp illuminates the dining area. Appliances have been painted with spray enamel in colors to match the walls.

2 A theatrical and beautifully contrasting effect. In this high-ceilinged contemporary space where black dominates, a grand traditional chandelier with hundreds of crystals hangs harmoniously next to very simple pendant lamps.

1

CHOOSING A TABLE

Don't be afraid to select a large table, because it's very likely to become a multifunctional center for the family: it's a place to pore over large books, to catch up on work, a place where the kids can have their snacks before doing their homework, and it will accommodate a lively group of friends comfortably. For dining, you need to count on about 28 inches for each table setting. For ten people, you will then need your table to measure at least six and a half feet long by five feet wide. Some find round tables more convivial, which is true as long as the table is not too big—a table for eight is about the limit.

If you find that a large table takes up too much space, opt for a smaller table with extensions. They can fold out at each end, or an extra leaf can be inserted in the middle. A clever solution is to put two tables, or even four, of the same type together to make one large table when needed.

Once you've figured out table size, you need to decide on a material. If your table will be located between the kitchen and the living room, make sure that it doesn't look out of place in either area. You don't have to be a slave to the "total look," which is completely outdated, especially in a loft. As always, it is a matter of taste. If you like rough wood, look for an old farm table at the secondhand shops, which you can easily maintain by washing with bleach. If you prefer a nice mahogany table, you should varnish it with care and protect it during meals. Contemporary wooden tables have generally already been given a protective coating. Glass is interesting; it makes the room look bigger, since it allows light to pass through it. Synthetic material has the advantage of being very easy to take care of. Lava stone, which comes in a wide range of colors, is solid and easy to take care of, but it's expensive. Some cover their tabletops with stainless steel. Another trendy idea, which goes well in a loft, is slate. If your kitchen is completely open to the eating area, you can make your tabletop from the same material as your counters.

CHOOSING CHAIRS

Don't hesitate to mix styles. You can pull metal office chairs up to a farm table, marry school or bistro chairs to a resin table, arrange iron chairs around a table covered in tile. You can also mix types of chairs, or paint them different colors. On the other hand, a coordinated table and chair ensemble can be very chic: why not an ensemble in blond wood, in rattan, or in wrought iron? For your barstools, tractor seats and hospital chairs can compete with bistro chairs. And for more comfort, choose models with backs.

1 Comfortable upholstered chairs and a stylish bamboo partition.
2 For entertaining, bistro-style wood bar stools.
3 Very decorative chairs in a boxy modern design.
4 An alliance of wood, metal, and plastic.
5 A beautiful sectional table made of several units.

1

2

3

4

5

EXTRA SEATING

It is such a pity to find yourself without enough chairs. Think of stools and stackable chairs for groups, or folding canvas director's chairs with either wooden, metal, or plastic frames, which you can put away in a cupboard, in a corner, behind a curtain, or hang on the wall with hooks when they are not needed. Garden chairs can also hit the right note. And kitchen stepstools are always useful in a loft.

1 A contemporary chair and designer plates.
2 Ergonomic metal barstools.
3 Light-colored wood, dressed up with vibrant colors.

HOTEL AND INSTITUTIONAL DINNERWARE

In flea markets and vintage stores, you may have a chance to find groups of functional place settings, very simple trays, and sturdy tea- and coffeepots. Some bear the logos of prestigious palaces, boats, or railway companies, others advertise obscure seaside hotels. The English manufacture big ewers and trophy cups for sports clubs and yachting societies, solidly made of metal with the obligatory silver plating. Even a little dented, a little worn, they can be very attractive. Stroll through shops devoted to supplying restaurant and institutional dinnerware. Here too function predominates, and the absence of gratuitous aesthetics gives these dishes their value. It is just so easy to fall for these unpretentious objects, especially when they are such bargains—unbreakable, or almost unbreakable, glasses and carafes, bistro-style salt and pepper shakers, egg cups, bar supplies, and chafing dishes. And as for dishes, don't forget to look into the boutiques that sell white porcelain and china.

Stairs and Mezzanines

It can be taken for granted that loft dwellers are generally not too eager to wall in their hard-won open space. On the other hand, the high ceilings that characterize most of the old industrial spaces make horizontal divisions welcome: platforms, footbridges, and mezzanines, which can be reached by stairs, enlarge the floor surface of a loft, allow for better distribution of space, and serve to differentiate areas of activity and create intimate nooks below them.

There are a lot of advantages to a mezzanine. Not only does it break up the space, but it balances and animates it in an interesting way that makes things appear bigger. The introduction of varying structures and forms, of supplemental vertical and horizontal lines, give the loft genuine architectural interest and a unique personality. The mezzanine also offers a view giving spectacular perspectives on the entire loft space. It should be open on one or more sides, not hinder natural light, and can even have a low ceiling without the feeling of claustrophobia.

In a loft, stairs are a means not only of passing from one level to another, but also of demonstrating creativity. Think of New York fire escapes, of factory and workshop stairs, or even of the stairs that you have loved in country or seaside houses. Please yourself. Whether an audacious structure imposing its presence like a sculpture, or a discreet, even airy, wisp, whether it occupies as little space as possible or projects elegantly from the backdrop of the wall, a flight of stairs fully participates in the architecture of a place by expressing your personality.

The choice of stairs depends on many factors, notably what kind of space you have and where they need to be placed. You should probably get the advice of a professional. Nevertheless, if you are a good do-it-yourselfer you can probably find the stairs of your dreams in a kit from a factory.

STAIRCASE TYPES

The simplest is the straight stair, made of one flight that runs along a wall, and is attached to it for support. The steps, generally around six or seven inches in height, are fixed independently. If you lack storage space, you can use the space under the stairs to create cupboards or bookshelves, or even place a piece of furniture there.

Stairs with a single bend, or dogleg stairs, placed for the most part against a wall, make one 90-degree turn. Stairs with multiple flights are made of at least two sets of steps, separated by a landing. This style is easy to navigate, but takes up a lot of important room.

Spiral staircases, inscribed in a cylindrical space, are made of one central column from which the steps fan out. These don't need to be attached to a wall and can easily be installed in the center of a room or in a corner. They are the stairs of choice when space is tight, as they generally have a diameter of less than five feet. A tip: a spiral staircase works best for right-handed people when it turns counterclockwise.

If you have limited space to install stairs, an open staircase will do the job, but be very careful about this choice if you have young children in the house.

1 An elegant painted metal spiral staircase. Its reassuring guardrails made of parallel tubes are airy, almost invisible.

2 This staircase allows light to pass through its Triplex glass panels, horizontal for the steps and vertical for the balusters.

STAIRWAY MATERIALS

It seems that people who live in lofts have a penchant for metal staircases. Steel is the most sought after; perforated sheet metal has a nice look, but it is loud; aluminum, flexible and light, also has its followers; and polished or brushed stainless steel is now very trendy. Wrought iron, inspired by nineteenth-century architecture, also has its charm. However, wooden stairs, descendants of the stairs of traditional houses, are the easiest to find in DIY stores, and come in hard woods such as oak, beech, or elm. Another solution consists of marrying wood and metal. For example, the pilasters that the banister is attached to might be steel, while the stair treads are wood. But other materials are possible: stone, glass, concrete, and so on.

For straight stairs, it can be interesting to treat the risers to prevent monotony. You can paint them or cover them in tile, mosaic, wood, and so on.

No matter what form they take, concrete stairs can be covered in all manner of ways—rough wood, floating parquet, carpet, or a flexible floor covering like linoleum. Once your wood is in place, you should varnish it, wax it, or coat it with paint made for floors. Avoid color washes or decorative finishes, which are too fragile. If you have installed a soft flooring, place a nonskid strip on the lip of each step.

3 An austere and steep straight stairway lined with a very graphic metallic guardrail.

4 We return to the nineteenth century with this metal spiral staircase with ornamental lacework risers and banister of an original design.

THE MEZZANINE

Mezzanines can be found in a number of industrial spaces, most of the time they are prefabricated metal platforms that served as storage space for stock. Sometimes, the owner puts his office there so he can keep an eye on his employees. To construct a mezzanine that you can stand up in, you need to have a ceiling height of at least thirteen feet, if you plan to divide this height horizontally into two more or less equal parts. If you only have twelve-foot ceilings, you can construct a platform that will hold a guest bed, a small office, or a television space for the children. If the mezzanine is not very high, don't make it very big, or it will feel oppressive. If stairs lead to it, they should also be as discreet as possible; a simple open staircase, or even a captain's ladder, should do the trick. The treads should rest on twenty-inch beams, usually with a central reinforcement beam. Depending on the history of your loft and its original construction materials, you can choose a wooden or metal structure, or opt for masonry.

1 In maritime style, the stairs and the guardrail in painted metal anchor the space of this immense loft.
2 Several wooden steps lead up to a platform, from which ladder-like metal stairs rise, and then are elongated into a footbridge. Everything gives the impression of great lightness.

3 The exceptionally high ceiling of this loft allows for the creation of a large mezzanine, which serves as a comfortable living room.

BANISTERS AND HANDRAILS

These elements are not only an important security measure, but can play a significant aesthetic role as well. For a guardrail, count on about three feet, three inches from the stair treads. If you use balusters, space them four inches apart. Some people replace balusters with translucent or transparent acrylic panels, which resemble glass, or even with a grill or with perforated metal stretched between metal girders.

The more common banisters are of wood or of metal tubing painted in matte or gloss, which evoke ship passageways. For added warmth you can sheathe them in rubber. Another nice maritime element is metal cables. You can also show your originality with rigging, lacework metal, chains, and so on.

1 Like a piece of contemporary sculpture, this banister has quite a presence.
2 The emphasis here is on the harmony of colors, in which the stairs play an integral part.

3 A black staircase attached to a red wall makes for a wonderful marriage of contrasting colors.

The Bedroom

Originally, it was artists who started the loft trend. They lived and worked in a large space, and it never occurred to them to erect partitions to make bedrooms. If you live alone or as a couple, you can of course live in this manner. Since flexibility is one of the great advantages of a loft, you may be tempted to move your bed around on casters with the seasons, or just on a whim. Some architects have designed entire alcoves on casters, like a bed enclosed in a cabinet—in fact, a small room that you can move to the four corners of a loft, as long as you have a big enough space. Though the loft dweller balks at erecting vertical partitions, he is willing to structure his space with horizontal divisions, and he will happily place his bed on a mezzanine.

This theoretical freedom, however, rarely stands up to the dictates of common sense. Most people prefer to sleep in the same place, in a serene, comfortable space genuinely dedicated to sleeping. In addition, lofts have to adapt to the demands of family life by preserving a modicum of intimacy for both parents and children. Therefore, the return to a closed space is inevitable. Fortunately, the principle of movable partitions gives us a way to restore perspective and volume to the loft during the day.

If you do create a genuine sleeping area, you can set its ambience off from that of the rest of the loft by playing with color. Allow yourself to be seduced by the serenity of white, make your room sunny with a cheery yellow, or enjoy the calm, cool feeling of green or blue. If the space does not have natural light or if you are a night owl, choose warm, deep colors. Another advantage to a closed-off bedroom is that it is easier to keep it clean. The loft allows for what many consider to be a luxury: a lot of storage space. Dressers, shelves, and boxes and crates multiply to allow us to conceal all but what we want to display.

THE NOMADIC BED

If, following the example of some loft dwellers, you consider that a bedroom is a waste of space, you can always sleep like the Japanese on a futon. At night, you unfold it; during the day you fold it back up and store it away or turn it into a sofa. This Japanese style of life is attractive, but restrictive: to save time and make your life easier are certainly among your priorities. The bed on casters (this being the best ally of the loft dweller, never skimp on its quality) also has its followers: you roll it into the middle of the room, you push it back against a wall . . .

THE SEDENTARY BED

Most people, however, prefer the intimate atmosphere of a real bedroom, whether it has the asceticism of a Zen space or is the center of many activities. The bed, once in place, doesn't budge. If your bedroom has natural light, don't place your bed directly under a window, for obvious reasons of temperature and comfort; instead, place it parallel to the window, so the sun won't be in your eyes, and if possible, install it opposite the entrance, or to one side of it.

1 In the guise of a headboard, a large monochrome panel hangs on the wall like a painting.

THE SLEEPING PLATFORM

In a somewhat vast rectangular space, you may have the urge to raise your bed on a platform about fifteen inches high, to be reached with a few steps. This not only makes a nice impression, but it creates storage possibilities as well. You could install drawers on the sides, or a trap door on top that would give you access to the entire space below.

THE SLEEPING MEZZANINE

If you want to put your bed on a mezzanine, your ceilings will need to be at least thirteen feet high, unless you will only be using the mezzanine for occasional sleeping or for children, in which case it will not be necessary to provide enough space to stand on the mezzanine. Consult a professional to know which type of mezzanine and stairs are best, what material is most appropriate, whether the walls are solid enough to hold the structure, and how much loadbearing capacity you need.

2 An occasional bed is placed on a mezzanine inundated with light. Sleepwalkers beware . . .

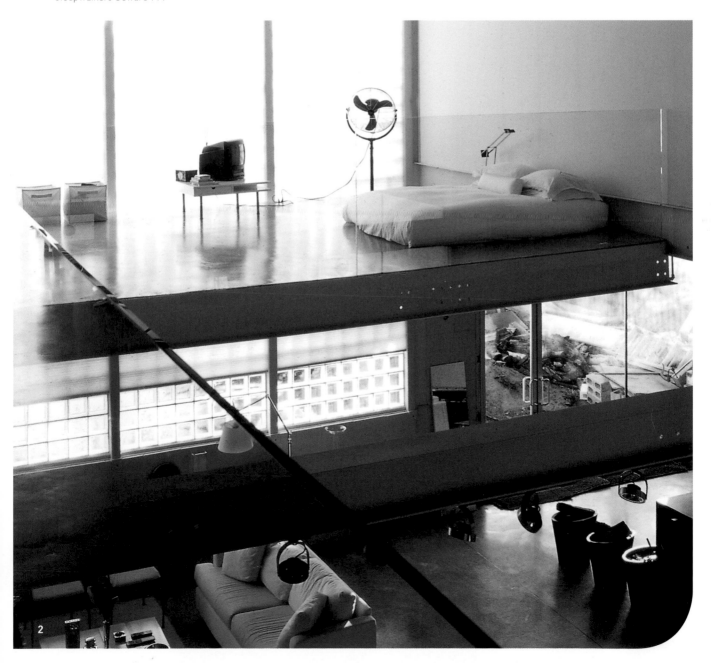

PARTITIONS

One of the great advantages of a loft is not having walls. Though some might be daring enough to set a bathtub in the middle of the room, however, many prefer to compromise by separating the bedroom from the bathroom with sliding partitions or fixed half walls. The same goes for separating the bedroom from the living area.

Large sliding panels of frosted glass, translucent plastic, or mirrored glass, mounted on rails, allow the space to remain open during the day, while closing off the bathroom from the bedroom when it is in use. Japanese screens, with their graphic cross-ruling, can be found today not only in translucent paper but also in resin, so they can be used in more humid places. Fixed screens are an all-purpose solution. They can be made in a variety of materials—wood, cloth, frosted glass, or metal—but remember that the more transparent the screen is, the more natural light it allows into the bathroom.

If you are looking for good soundproofing between the bathroom and the bedroom, construct a partition of glass bricks, which have the added advantage of letting light through. A half-height masonry wall placed behind the bed can hide a part of the bathroom while also serving as a headboard.

1 To diminish the effect of a corridor and accentuate the perspective, bands of color have been painted on the floor, echoing the paintwork around the doors.

2 Movable transparent panels assure thermal and sound insulation for this bedroom. Large industrial radiators run along a glass wall.

1

BEDSIDE TABLES AND LAMPS

The old bedside table has been relegated to the rank of useless antique; they are never a good height, are too small, hardly practical, and incompatible with a good lamp. You don't need a lot of space to construct, behind the bed, a box that projects on both sides so as to act as both a headboard and a side table. Shelves or cubbies, set at a proper height, can hold lamps, a clock radio, books, and photos. If you want a bedside lamp, contemporary models are quite adaptable. Sometimes a shelf placed at the right height will suffice for indispensable objects and clamp-on lamps that can be adjusted to different angles. In a loft, though, anything goes: pharmacy furniture, hospital side tables with adjustable arms—the list goes on.

For lighting, combine sources of ambient light—flush-fitting ceiling lights, wall sconces, spotlights—with reading lamps. Choose adjustable lamps with dimmers, which are the least likely to disturb a sleeping partner, and place them about two feet above the bed. Don't forget to install two-way switches, so that bedroom lighting can be switched on and off from the entrance of the room as well as from the bed.

1 In this somewhat baroque bedroom, an Indian trunk in dark wood is used as a bedside table and holds a large faience lamp.

2 The bedroom is separated from the bathroom by a deep wooden cupboard on which is placed a lamp for ambient light.

2

THE CLOSET

Save from the point of view of nostalgia, Grandmother's wardrobe is a thing of the past; today there are far more functional solutions. The ideal is to have a real closet; that is, a piece custom-made for your needs. There are also more economical choices. As always when you have to store things, make a merciless inventory of all that you want to keep, and then determine the number of shelves and drawers and the length of rail you think you will need, rounding up so that you avoid the nightmare of having to cram everything in. If you can devote a wall to storage, install a permanent modular system, with a steel, iron, or less expensive wooden framework running the length of the wall from floor to ceiling, and equip it with hanging units, drawers, and adjustable shelves (it should be at least two feet deep, to accommodate hangers). An idea to save space is a swing-down clothes rack, in which two clothes rods are mounted one above the other—the top rail, hinged by attachments to the wall, has a vertical handle that can be grasped to pull it forward and down within reach when needed. You can close off closet systems with sliding doors: these can be painted the same color as the walls so they blend in, or they can be translucent, mirrored, or even made of a series of curtains on a rod. A bit of advice: you might want to put broad, swiveling load-bearing casters on your closet doors to make them easier to open and close. On clothes rods, in addition to clothes, you can suspend a series of small flexible shelves for underwear, scarves, and socks, unless you prefer to keep them in baskets or drawers.

1 Drawers cleverly fashioned in the risers of steps.

2 Original and witty, this clothes storage system installed in the bedroom is made of wooden boxes suspended from a bar.

ADDITIONAL STORAGE

For those things that you do not use every day, trunks on casters or carefully labeled boxes can do the trick. Storing shoes can be a problem. Yes, of course, storage units exist that are designed specifically for them, but you can also try pairs of locker-room hooks, concealed behind a curtain; wooden shelves, like a CD rack, each containing a pair of shoes; or shoe boxes, each labeled or with a photo of the shoes attached.

UNDER-BED STORAGE

Think of using the space under your bed, it's very practical for storing blankets, comforters, and sometimes off-season clothing, either in chests with casters or in drawers that pull out from the sides or foot of the bed. If the bed is high enough, slide a platform on casters under it on which you can place, for example, your empty suitcases. Finally, designers have conceived of an electric system placed at the head of the bed that permits your mattress, which is attached to a platform, to swing up to allow access to a large chest underneath.

THE SPIRIT OF SALVAGING

In matters of efficient storage, warehouses, workshops, and stores can teach us all a lesson, and their functional systems work marvelously in lofts. You might be able to find a bargain in metal cabinets like those found in school locker rooms, barracks, or airport baggage rooms. Think also of factory furniture with small drawers, artisans' furniture, toolboxes, metal chests on casters, stackable plastic boxes, office files, and the like.

1 A grand wooden wardrobe provides efficient organization.
2 A large space devoted to storage is cleverly hidden behind sliding doors with wood frames.
3 An assortment of wooden cabinets and drawers without handles line the wall in this bedroom.
4 Everything in its place: here underwear is neatly folded in a compartmented drawer.

2

3

4

TAMING LIGHT

Light often comes into lofts not through ordinary windows but through large expanses of glass. If this is the case in your bedroom, you may want to protect yourself not only from the exposure of bright light but also from the eyes of others. In this case, there are many solutions to choose from.

One is to treat the windowpane itself. It is possible to replace transparent panes with frosted glass, in part of the window or in the whole thing. If you do not want curtains or blinds, you can cover the window glass with translucent or colored PVC films; these permit you to see outside without being seen and protect against ultraviolet radiation, a valuable quality if you want to protect your artwork, fabrics, or carpets. Since they exist in various colors, you can go wild: it's no trouble to change them if you tire of them.

SHEERS

Sheer curtains work quite well for bedrooms. Depending on how exposed your window is to outside view, you can run a taut metal wire (of a length up to fifteen feet or so) across the window at mid height and string airy muslin, cotton, or extra fine linen curtains pierced with small eyelets along it. Otherwise, install airy streams of fabric that will ripple in the softest breeze, the full height of the window, on thin rods. For a more clean-lined effect, opt for sliding panels placed in front of the window (but make sure they don't make it difficult to open the window).

1 The bedroom is separated from the bathroom by white linen curtain pierced with metal-rimmed grommets, threaded on a metal rod and elegantly flowing down over the wooden floor.

2 Inundated with light, this white-on-white bedroom exudes serenity. A simple curtain slid onto a rod shields it from the outside world.

CURTAINS

Curtains have their charm in a loft, and their substantial fabric guarantees good insulation. In addition to buffering light, they can also soften a more severe look or set off the bedroom, or even just the bed (make sure that they slide quickly and easily). You can choose from a number of materials, including flannel, tweed, hemp, ticking, contemporary fabric, and, for a bit more drama, velvet. If you prefer a light fabric, which goes well with the serenity of a bedroom, a double layer will block the light better. If you like to tie curtains back, use your imagination: cords, twine, vines, ethnic necklaces, and string are only a few ideas.

BLINDS

If you have large picture windows, it might be interesting to install several blinds side by side—and why not use different widths? You have the choice between many types. There are very simple wind-up blinds (if you opt for light fabric, you will need to starch it). Roman blinds, with large horizontal pleats, go well with the clean look of a loft; they can be made not only of natural materials like cotton, linen, vegetable fibers like raffia, bamboo, banana, or hemp, but also of contemporary materials like spinnaker cloth, fiberglass, woven metal, or PVC. Venetian blinds, descended from shutters, are made of horizontal wooden, metal, or plastic slats and are distinctly preferred by architects, since they produce an especially graphic play of light and dark shadows reflected onto the floor or a wall.

1 Absolute simplicity: a Roman blind invisibly attached to a white wall.

2 The flow of natural light that penetrates this bedroom from the immense picture window is nicely tamed by plastic venetian blinds.

The Bathroom

The bathroom has been transformed in recent years. The cult of the body, the tendency toward hedonism, the development of hydrotherapy and hydromassage, to say nothing of aromatherapy (well-being from herbs and essential oils) and chromotherapy (well-being from color)—all this has made the bathroom a place where we spend more and more time, a room devoted not only to hygiene but also to health and relaxation. The bathroom is not hidden away as it used to be; on the contrary, it is exposed to view, with its efficient plumbing, its accessories, its subtle lighting, and its thick towels that evoke a universe of luxury.

Of course, not all these facilities are within everyone's reach, but a multijet shower, for example, is quite affordable. Add to that a bit of imagination and some cleverness, and everyone can have a dream bathroom.

The loft, with its wealth of space, can accommodate a large bathroom that receives a lot of natural light. Depending on your own taste, you can opt for the purity of a Zen style, a severe high-tech institutional look, or the subjective expression of your own personality.

Open or closed? That really just depends on the number of people who will be using the bathroom. A solution for a single person is to have a partition that serves as a headboard for the bed on one side, while concealing the plumbing for a washstand or bathtub on the other. A couple should consider their respective schedules and how much intimacy they each need. And for more than two people, the bathroom needs to be independent from the bedroom, or it will prove a constant inconvenience.

Whichever option you choose, there are a few absolute requirements: humidity-resistant material that is easy to maintain, attention to lighting, and elementary rules of safety. As for the rest, anything is possible.

TILE

High marks for this material, which is ideal for bathrooms. Durable and easy to keep clean, it comes in a range of materials and colors, and in a wide range of prices. There are tiles for walls, less-trafficked floors, and passageways. For example, faience is only used on walls; polished stone works for both bathroom walls and floors; ceramic tile is tougher, and thus can even be used for exteriors.

Today's trend for bathroom walls and tub enclosures, which is especially appropriate for lofts, is tile that imitates granite, slate, earth, and sand. These tiles can be used as a contrasting trim for walls and floors done in tile in plain white or cream. White tile also has its diehard fans. You can play with different tile shapes and sizes to break the monotony, combining, for instance, flat squares and rectangular subway tile. If you prefer color, your choice is unlimited. You might be tempted by checkerboard effects, monochrome designs, a play of contrasting colors, friezes, motifs, mosaics . . .

PAINTWORK

If you do not want to hide U-bends or pipes, if you don't want your bathroom to be a small replica of Beaubourg, if you consider that it is a room to live in like any other, you will probably decide to paint its walls, an economical solution, in any case. Depending on your taste, you can use a single color, or you can play with nuances and contrasts. In all cases, avoid water-based paint and go for satin or gloss oil-based paint that can be cleaned with a simple wipe of a sponge. Remember that you will first have to coat your walls with a universal primer. However, paint is not ideal for surfaces that are always in contact with water, so you will need to plan on painting half of the wall and choose another covering for the lower part of the walls, which will be prone to getting splashed.

WOOD

A bathroom entirely in wood, or simply with wood wainscoting, is warm and comfortable as long as you choose naturally decay-resistant woods like iroko, merbeau, ipe, or teak, which are also suited for shower units, the floor, or washbasins. Without treatment, they have a tendency to turn gray, so if you want them to retain their original color, use a rag to coat them with several coats of teak oil. It will of course be necessary to repeat this treatment regularly.

Laminated wood flooring—attached to a synthetic resin support that is waterproof—is an excellent solution for humid rooms, and you can also choose among different species like oak, beech, or pine, whichever best suits the effect you want.

MOSAIC

These tiny glass tiles have captivated many designers and architects. They come in a number of solid colors as well as in monochrome designs, in metallic gold or silver, or

1 High drama: an antique clawfoot bathtub, all dressed in black.

in clear glass. Each tile measures three-quarters of an inch square, with a thickness of an eighth of an inch, and they come in sheets that are about three feet square. They are difficult to lay; grouting them, particularly, is an exacting task, especially on floors, and would be best done by a professional.

PEBBLES

If you don't have a chance to collect these out in nature, you can find pebbles mounted in square sheets, in varying colors—anthracite, light gray, beige, or pink. They make quite an effect, but if you have sensitive feet, it's better to restrict their use to the edges of the floor. On the walls, use them to create geometric motifs in friezes, or as a decorative trim.

1 In an austere spirit, the light wooden floor used throughout the loft effectively sets off the slate used to surround the bathroom fixtures.

2 A group of informally clustered surf-worn stones, collected from the beach, animates this bathroom, where the tub resembles a small boat.

SCULPTURAL BATHTUBS

If you opt for an old-fashioned bathroom, you can track down an old copper or iron tub, usually on claw feet, at a salvage store that you can have reenameled. It will look nice in a loft, especially if you dare to put it in the middle of the room (if there is enough space in the floor for the pipes, that is). To optimize the effect, you can find a replicate of the classic old faucet with its cross-shaped handle, a porcelain knob in the center marked "hot" and "cold." Don't feel obligated to find an old washstand. An old tub can easily go with a contemporary basin.

If you want your tub to be the focal point of your bathroom, budget permitting, you can choose among contemporary models, often generous in size, that are veritable sculptures. These can be molded of synthetic resin or acrylic, or constructed in wood, like a sauna.

HYDROMASSAGE SYSTEMS

Hydrotherapy, a wonderful resource for relaxation and pleasure, is a fairly recent development. Hydromassage systems are becoming more accessible, more efficient, and quieter. For these to work properly, you will need a relatively large bathtub (six feet long and very wide). Different systems are available. The simplest is with air, which creates a whirlpool when pushed out from the bottom of the bathtub. The object is not to give a deep massage, but to relax one in a bath of effervescent bubbles.

A second system uses both air and water. The water of the bath is circulated and, mixed with air, passes through ducts placed at the back of the bathtub, at back level; on the sides, by the legs; and at the front, near the feet. The jets soothe away muscle tension and have a massage and tonic effect.

A third system, the most sophisticated, combines air, water, and ultrasound, for a profound massage that may even have an effect on cellular metabolism.

1 This architectural bathroom, entirely encased in light-hued wood, has a warm saunalike atmosphere.
2 A functional aesthetic: one solid block of synthetic resin, with varying levels and cutout spaces that give it a sculptural effect.

THE SHOWER

For those addicted to showers, there is no shortage of solutions. If you have enough space, the ideal is to construct a shower cubicle in masonry, lined in tile, in faience, or in glass bricks, and deep enough so that there is no need to close it off with a door panel or curtain. Here, you can install a custom-designed hydromassage system, with jets placed in ideal positions on all sides, which can mimic rain and create enough steam for a genuine Turkish bath.

If this solution is not possible, and you have only a small amount of space, you can opt for a completely waterproof, closed-off shower cubicle equipped with hydromassage. There are also corner shower units, and others are adaptable to roof spaces or come with a bathtub. In any kind of shower unit, you can install a hydromassage column with all the necessary accessories: nozzles overhead and at back or pelvis level, as well as shelves, and perhaps even a seat. The only requirement is that you have an ample supply of water and good water pressure.

1 A spectacular shower equipped with a high-tech hydromassage system rises from the center of this immense bathroom that communicates directly with the bedroom.

BASINS AND SINKS

Basins today are so attractive that they deserve to be on display, sometimes in pairs. At the top of the list you'll find ceramic basins, transparent or opaque glass, translucent or colored resin, enameled iron, stainless steel, chrome, acrylic, and enameled lava stone. As attractive as round shapes can be, commercial sinks, such as one finds in institutions, are sought out for their severe, functional lines; you can also find a softer interpretation of this style, with rounded edges and soft slopes.

When a basin is simply placed on a counter, its form and material can contrast with those of its support to great effect: thus, the whiteness of an acrylic basin

heightens the effect of dark gray tile, and a metal basin sets off a glass countertop.

Another solution is to sink a basin into a flat counter (this works best if the visible pipes are attractive); or find a unit that combines basin and counter in one seamless block, a very clean, sleek look, in glass or ceramic. These one-piece units can either stand on legs or be fixed directly to the wall, if it is sturdy enough to support them.

The third solution is to set basins into a piece of cabinetry that forms a suite with the bathtub and other bathroom fixtures.

1 To save space, this rectangular basin is set in the corner of two walls on a dark wooden cabinet.

2 A round basin attached directly to the wall, giving it an overall air of lightness.

1

2

FAUCETS

At its purest, the hardware for the sink can be reduced to a pair of separate faucets with round or cross-shaped handles, or ending in a colored knob, preferably mounted on the wall for a fountainlike effect and to make upkeep easier. For the bathtub as well, this system allows for rapid flow, but the mixing faucet is more practical and economical.

A thermostatic mixing faucet, which avoids disagreeable variations of temperature, is the most adaptable for a shower and the safest for children. As for shower heads, they range from a simple tube pierced with holes through its length—very high design—and the traditional large shower heads, to shower heads that adjust to three different massaging jet streams, diffuse or raining down. For both practical and aesthetic reasons, it is preferable, whenever possible, to encase the fixtures in an absolutely waterproof way in the wall or partition.

HEATED TOWEL RACKS

It is a true small pleasure to wrap yourself in a warm towel after a bath or shower. The heated towel rack is essentially a radiator, which has the advantage of providing extra warmth in the bathroom while it warms and dries towels. Electrical models are available that can be either hard-wired or plugged in; hydronic models, which may need to be installed by a plumber, use the loft's main hot-water system. They are available as freestanding floor units or wall-mounted racks, with shelves or round or flattened tubes in a variety of configurations. Heated towel racks can be found in every possible color, as well as chrome. Their industrial style adapts ideally to loft bathrooms. The most luxurious versions may incorporate extras like a mirror, storage space, or even a bench to sit on as well.

1 Reminiscent of a public drinking fountain, this fixture is mounted on the wall. The water flows into the columnar metal basin.
2 A salvaged hospital faucet, made for washing hands in an operating room, finds a new life in this loft.
3 In this magnificent bathroom with its massive bathtub enthroned on a wooden platform, the shower is hidden behind glass bricks.

CABINETS AND STORAGE

What a number of things, even if they are small, there are to arrange in a bathroom! The best way is to sort them by type. Thus, aspirin, prescriptions, first aid supplies, and the like would be placed in their own cupboard with a lock; cosmetics need a shallow cabinet or open shelves if you do not choose to keep them in a dressing table, which can be very practical. In any case, something with drawers is needed for lipstick, nail polish, hair care products, and so on. If you prefer to have most of these things close at hand, consider trays or hanging containers: you can keep your hair dryer, brushes, and combs there. Piles of thick towels have considerable eye appeal. You can stack them under the

sink on a glass shelf, for example, since they take up a lot of room. Or, if you have the necessary space, you can construct a series of deep shelves out of masonry, covered with the material of your choice. Whatever you do, it is best to adapt the storage units to the configuration of the room, to take advantage of niches, slopes, and corner shelving. Some storage units intended for the kitchen are perfect for the bathroom; try, for example, produce baskets on casters, rails, or metal grids with hooks, from which you can hang cloth bags or metal containers, buckets, pots, boxes, and jars. A footstool with a storage compartment can prove invaluable.

1 Towels are stacked under the basin on an open shelf, or hung on a particularly practical metal bar.

2 The basin of this sink rests on an extra-deep cabinet, made of the same two types of wood used for the bathroom floor and steps.

3 A large basket for towels and four small ones for accessories slide under the basin, their rough natural material making a striking contrast to the metal of the sink cabinet.

LIGHTING

Even if it enjoys natural illumination throughout the day, a bathroom needs carefully thought-out lighting, since it is most often used at night or in the early morning. The principle is the same as for the other rooms of the house: combine ambient illumination with targeted lighting. Low-wattage recessed spotlights are a good and very cheap solution, especially if you have them on a dimmer. Thus, you can have them dimmed to a soft glow when you want to relax in the bathtub, which you can complete with some candles for ambience, and turned up high in the morning, when you are pressed to get ready for the day. You can also seek out wall sconces, or install spots on rails. For shaving and putting on makeup, lighting should be bright and flattering, and not cast shadows. You might install a vertical light fixture on each side of the mirror, or surround it with a number of frosted bulbs that light without blinding. Bathroom cabinets often come with well-designed built-in lighting, or halogen or incandescent spotlights.

1 A skylight in the ceiling of this bathroom lets in natural light. The mirror is equipped with a lamp.

2 Natural light for the day, spotlights for the nighttime.

1

Address Book

2MODERN
38 Miller Avenue #221
Mill Valley CA 94941
Tel: 888-222-4410
www.2modern.com
furnishings and accessories

ANN SACKS
8120 NE 33rd Drive
Portland, OR 97211
Tel: 800-278-8453

CRATE AND BARREL
Stores located across the US
Tel: 800-967-6696
www.crateandbarrel.com
home furnishings and accessories

DESIGN PUBLIC
300 Brannan Street
Suite 403
San Francisco, CA 94107
Tel: 800-506-6541
www.designpublic.com

DESIGN WITHIN REACH
Studios located across the US
Tel: 800-944-2233
www.dwr.com
contemporary furnishings and design

FORM + FUNCTION
851 West San Mateo Road
Santa Fe, New Mexico 87505
USA
Tel: 800-264-0057
www.formplusfunction.com
lighting

GOLD MEDAL DESIGN
2151 Murray Hill Road
Cleveland, OH 44106
Tel: 216-791-1435
Fax: 520-244-2506
specializes in loft interior designs

IKEA
Stores located in more than 30 countries and across the US
www.ikea.com
contemporary furniture and designs

LIGHTOLOGY
1718 West Fullerton Ave.
Chicago, IL 60614
Tel: 866-954-4489
Fax: 773-883-6131
www.lightology.com
lighting

MANHATTAN LOFT
2358 South Main St.
Salt Lake City, UT 84115
Tel: 877-511-0400
www.manhattanloft.com
contemporary furniture and designs

MARIA BELL INTERIOR DESIGNS
800 Duboce #204
San Francisco, California 94117
Tel: 415-431-9474
specializes in loft interior design

MARMOLEUM
Forbo Flooring
PO Box 667 Humboldt Ind. Park
Hazelton, PA 18201
Tel: 570-459-0771
flooring

POTTERY BARN
Stores across the US and in Canada
www.potterybarn.com
home furnishings and accessories

ROOM & BOARD
Stores located across the US
Tel: 800-301-9720
www.roomandboard.com

SONOMA CAST STONE
PO Box 1721
Sonoma, CA 95476
Tel: 888-807-4234
www.sonomacaststone.com

WATERWORKS
Stores located across the US
Tel: 800-998-BATH
www.waterworks.com

WEST ELM
Stores located across the US
Tel: 888-922-4119
www.westelm.com
contemporary furniture and designs

WILLIAMS-SONOMA
Stores located across the US and
Canada
Tel: 877-812-6235
www.williams-sonoma.com
home furnishings and accessories

UNITED KINGDOM

ALTITUDELOFTS
24-26 Fournier St
London E1 6QE
UK
Tel: +44 (0) 20 73772838
www.altitudelofts.co.uk
loft conversions and interior design

AMTICO INTERNATIONAL
Solar Park
Southside
Solihull
West Midlands
B90 4SH
UK
Tel: +44 (0) 8703 504080
www.amtico.co.uk
tiles, flooring

ARAM
110 Drury Lane
Covent Garden
London WC2B 5SG
UK
Tel: +44 (0) 20 7557 7557
Fax: +44 (0) 20 7557 7558
www.aram.co.uk
designer furniture

BHS
Stores located throughout the UK
Tel: +44 (0) 845 196 00 00
www.bhs.co.uk
furniture, home furnishings, accessories

BODO SPERLEIN LTD.
Unit 1.05
OXO Tower Wharf
Barge Street, London SE1 9PF
UK
Tel: +44 (0) 20 7633 9413
www.bodosperlein.com
design consultancy and manufacturers of lighting, furniture, giftware, china

CHRISTOPHER WRAY
Stores located throughout England
Tel: +44 (0) 20 7751 8701
Fax: +44 (020) 7751 8699
www.christopher-wray.com
classic and contemporary furniture, lighting

CRITERION#2 TILES
(formerly Tile Reject Shop)
178 Wandsworth Bridge Road
London SW6 2UQ
Tel: +44 (0) 20 7731 6098
Fax: +44 (0) 20 7736 3693
www.criterion-tiles.co.uk
wide range of new and slight seconds in tiles of all sorts

ECLECTICS
1 Poorhole Lane
Kent CT10 2PP
UK
Tel: +44 (0) 870 010 2211
Fax: +44 (0) 1843 608797
www.eclectics.co.uk
contemporary blinds, screens, room dividers, made to measure

HABITAT
Stores located throughout the UK
Tel: +44 (0) 20 7351 1211
www.habitat.net/uk
contemporary furniture and home furnishings, kitchen accessories

HEAL'S
Stores located in major cities in the
UK
Tel: +44 (0) 20 7636 1666
www.heals.co.uk
contemporary furniture and accessories

HOMEFRENZY FURNITURE AND LIGHTING
Unit 10
Evans Business Centre
Albion Way, Leeds LS12 2EJ
UK
Tel: +44 (0) 870 720 0098
www.homefrenzy.com
furniture, storage, mirrors, lighting

JOHN LEWIS
Stores located throughout the UK
Tel: +44 (0) 8456 049 049
www.johnlewis.co.uk
high street department store with furni-
ture, furnishings, accessories

LIBERTY
Regent Street
London W1
UK
Tel: +44 (0) 20 7734 1234
Fax: +44 (0) 20 7573 9898
classic English fabrics and home furnishings

LOFT CONVERSION WAREHOUSE LTD.
9 Motcomb Street
London SW1X 8LA
UK
Tel: +44 (0) 20 7245 1150
Fax: +44 (0) 20 7201 2569
www.loftconversionwarehouse.com
architectural design and decorating services

MARTIN BARNETT FURNITURE
68 Marylebone Lane
London W1U 2PQ
UK
Tel: +44 (0) 20 7487 2997
Fax: +44 (0) 20 7487 2717
www.martinbarnett.co.uk/home.php
exclusive designer furniture

NEW HEIGHTS
Stores located throughout the UK
Tel: +44 (0) 20 8452 1500
www.new-heights.co.uk
contemporary wood furniture, storage
solutions

NEXT
Stores located throughout the UK
Tel: +44 (0) 845 600 7000
www.next.co.uk
department store carrying furniture, home
furnishings, lighting, storage

OCEAN DESIGN FOR CONTEMPORARY LIVING
Ocean Sunrise Ltd.
Unit 17
Spectrum House
32–34 Gordon House Road
London NW5 1LP
UK
Tel: +44 (0) 870 242 6283
www.ocean-furniture.co.uk
modern and classic furniture and furnishings

POP UK CONTEMPORARY FURNITURE, LIGHTING AND ACCESSORIES
278 Upper Richmond Road
Putney, London SW15 6TQ
UK
Tel: +44 (0) 20 8788 8811
Fax: +44 (0) 20 8788 2244
www.popuk.com
contemporary design shop for furniture,
lighting, accessories

PORCELANOSA
Stores located throughout the UK
Tel: +44 (0) 208 680 1123
Fax: +44 (0) 8702 240 245
www.porcelanosa.co.uk
contemporary bathroom furniture and
accessories

WORLD'S END TILES
Silverthorne Road
Battersea London SW8 3HE
UK
Tel: +44 (0) 20 7819 2110
Fax: +44 (0) 20 7819 2101
www.worldsendtiles.co.uk

HONG KONG

ARTEMIDE LTD
Shop 111
Ruttonjiee Centre
11 Duddell Street
Central - Hong Kong
Tel.: +852 2523 0333 or 2882 6863
Fax: +852 2845 0544 or 2882 6866
info@artemide.com.hk
lighting

AVA FURNITURE CO LTD
2/F, 55–57 Wang Lung St
Leitz Ind Bldg, Tsuen Wan
New Territories, Hong Kong
Tel: +852 2409 4480
Fax: +852 2409 6465
a sleek range of minimalist home furniture

FIRED EARTH
2404 Dominion Centre
43–59 Queens Road East
Wanchai, Wanchai
Hong Kong
Tel: +852 2861 3864
Fax: +852 2865 7300
Email: mrmconst@netvigator.com
www.firedearth.com
*handmade painted and plain floor and
wall tiles, stone, terracotta and natural
floorings*

**MADISON (HONG KONG) LTD.
SHOP A, LOWER GROUND
FLOOR**
Ruttonjee Centre, 11 Duddell Street
Central - Hong Kong
Tel: +852 2868 9323
Fax: +852 2345 7936
sales@bulthaup.com.hk
www.bulthaup.com (see for various
other locations including UK)
*specialize in creating kitchens with modu-
lar elements for small spaces*

**QIANTANG RIVER ARTS &
FURNITURE LTD**
20/F, Goodwill Ind Bldg
36–44 Pak Tin Par St, Tsuen Wan
New Territories, Hong Kong
Tel: +852 2492 0165
Fax: +852 2411 1025
*specializes in pieces on the traditional end
of the stylistic spectrum, with a collection
of Chinese-style wooden furniture as well
as porcelain and ceramic objects*

**TEAM HC LIMITED
ARCHITECTURE AND DESIGN**
10A Dotcom House
126 Wellingon Street
Central-Hong Kong
Tel.: +852 2581 2011
Fax: +852 2581 0279
www.teamhc.com
architecture, design, interiors, furniture

AUSTRALIA AND
NEW ZEALAND

INNERSPACE INTERIOR DESIGN
493 High St
Prahran East VIC 3181
Australia
Tel: +61 3 9510 7946
Fax: +61 3 9510 7413
www.innerspaceinteriors.com.au
*interior design combining classical and
contemporary styles, custom furniture*

BOS DESIGN
422 Dominion Road, Mt Eden
Auckland, New Zealand
Tel: +64 9 638 6756
Fax: +64 0 623 1705
www.bosdesign.co.nz

DAVID JONES
310 Bourke Street
Melbourne 3000
Australia
Tel: +61 3 9643 2222
Fax: +61 3 9643 2000
www.davidjones.com.au
*department store carrying contemporary
furniture, home furnishings*

**HUB FURNITURE LIGHTING
LIVING**
63 Exhibition Street
Melbourne Vic 3000
Australia
Tel: +61 3 9650 1366
www.hubfurniture.com.au
*international contemporary furniture, light-
ing and living*

KATALOG
Showroom & Office
24 Spring Street, Freemans Bay
Auckland, New Zealand
Tel.: +64 9 360 4290
Fax: +64 9 360 4291
www.katalog.co.nz
*contemporary design furniture, lighting,
storage solutions*

Books

Bahamon, Alajandro, **SMALL LOFTS**. New York: Collins Design, 2005.

Banks, Orianna and Rebecca Tanqueray, **LOFTS: LIVING IN SPACE**. New York: Universe, 1999.

BIG BOOK OF LOFTS, Cologne: Taschen, 2005.

Broto, C., **DOMESTIC INTERIORS**. Barcelona: Links International, 2000.

Canizares, Ana G., **LOFTS DESIGN SOURCE**. New York: HarperCollins, 2004.

Cerver, Francisco Asensio, **LOFTS: A WAY OF LIVING, A WAY OF WORKING**. Barcelona: Atrium Group, 2002.

Cerver, Francisco Asensio, **LOFTS: LIVING AND WORKING SPACES**. New York: Watson-Guptill Publications, 1999.

Cuito, Aurora, **LOFTS: DESIGNER & DESIGN**. Madrid: H. Kliczkowski, 2003.

Cuito, Aurora, **LOFTS**. Harper Design, 2003.

Field, Marcus and Mark Irving, **LOFTS**. California: Gingko Press, 1999.

Molner, Felicia Eisenberg, **LOFTS: NEW DESIGNS FOR URBAN LIVING**. Gloucester, Massachusetts: Rockport Publishers, 1999.

Stone, Katherine, **LOFT DESIGN: SOLUTIONS FOR CREATING A LIVEABLE SPACE**. Massachusetts: Rockport Publishers, 2003.

Tolliver, Jessica, **LOFT STYLE**. Friedman/Fairfax, 1998.

Vance, Peggy, **LOFT LIVING**. London: Cassell, 2000.

Wilhide, Elizabeth, **NEW LOFT LIVING**. London: Carlton Books/New York: Universe, 2002.